Unveiling The Secret:

Practical Steps to Succeeding with The Law of Attraction!

By:

Annetta L. Hunter

Copyright © 2013 by Annetta L. Hunter & Transition Strategies. All rights reserved. The contents of this book shall not be copied without the prior permission from the author.

Transition Strategies
110 Waterford Lane
Glasgow, KY 42141

Annetta.hunter@gmail.com

Unveiling The Secret:

Practical Steps to Succeeding with The Law of Attraction!

By: Annetta L. Hunter

For all those who have gotten lost in their quest to achieve success

with

The Law of Attraction,

and

My gift to Christian and Taylor,

The manifested lights of my life!

I Love You!

Mommy

Contents

Introduction

Chapter 1
My Secret Revealed

Chapter 2
How to Decipher the Secret

Chapter 3
Unraveling and Erasing the Negative
Thoughts and Behaviors that Hold You Back!

Chapter 4
Immersion Technique is Key!

Chapter 5
It's A Mindset…Get your mind set to take Action!

Chapter 6
Creating your World…Create the Vision First!

Chapter 7
Vision Boards and Goals Oh My!

Chapter 8
Breaking Free to Finally Achieve your Dreams!

Chapter 9
Measure Your Success…Be Grateful for Everything

Chapter 10
Pass it On! Share the Secret with Others

Bonus Chapter
Recipe for The Law of Attraction

Introduction

It is interesting when one takes on something that is meant to be. The process is so easy and flows with anticipation of what comes next, and then you find it is finished! When I decided that I was going to write this book, I wondered if I would complete it, considering that I am famous for my incomplete writings! But, something in me knew that I had something important to say, something that would help others who were lost like I was and frustrated with The Law of Attraction not working for them. I knew somehow that this was going to get finished, and published. The information being offered is from my point of view and experiences with what works and what does not.

Learning more and more about The Law of Attraction and many other universal laws has been my awakening. I have been on a quest of "Self-Actualization" for many years, and finally, I believe that I am closer to knowing who I really am than ever before! It is exciting knowing that I can create the life I want to live; knowing that my choices mold and shape my experiences in this life, and that teaching this principle to my children will aid in their success early in life without wasting as much time as I did.

I was moved to share what I found out, because I know that I am not alone in this quest to know more about our existence on this earth and how to live the best life that we can. I want others to know the steps that I have taken to realize my dreams. It may not all be about great wealth, but about being happy; about being the best person that I can be, and be of service to others. Do not get me wrong, it is nice to have the wealth and all that comes with it, but ultimately, that is not going to make you happy. Having a strong spiritual walk and relationship with our Creator, doing what you love every day, even if you are not paid to do it is an amazing feeling! Bringing happiness and love to others and being a positive influence is also very satisfying. I have found that if you know what brings you joy, and you do work that fulfills that joy, your needs will be met. I have always strived to do work that I loved because it feeds my soul. I am a creative being. I enjoy the process and the dreaming of something and making it reality. Even when my father encouraged me to become an Engineer, something deep within me kept me on the path of what I loved most which was Architecture. We must know who we are and stay true to that person within in order to be happy and I would not change those decisions to be true to me for anything!

I have had several people in my life who inspired me and have lead me to this place, and one of the first ones who influenced me in attracting what I wanted in life were my parents. My father, who came from a poor family of six children and a single mother, who exceeded all expectations, to obtain a full Basketball Scholarship to Oklahoma City University, then realized his dream to become a pro-basketball player, drafted by the Boston Celtics in 1966! That was astounding considering the time period, his being African American, and from the little town he came from, that he was noticed by college scouts and was offered several prestigious scholarships to incredible schools, then, before graduating college was picked up by one, if not the most popular basketball team in the country! He has always been one of my inspirations!

Then, there is my mother. She continues to conjure up nearly whatever she desires and always has. I tell the story of her dream car in the book which is a true lesson in what not to do on one hand, but also how The Law of Attraction can work to the negative as well as to the positive! She manifested the beautiful homes we lived in, and many other things in life that she wanted came true through the use of The Law of Attraction. She did it so well in fact, she did not really even know she was doing it! Imagine what you can do with specific intention of using this law!

Not only great thinkers of yesterday, but the wonderful modern sages of today inspire new ideas of how to apply the Law of Attraction to my life. I have new dreams because of what I have learned from them, and what I have been able to realize in my life in the past! I know that they will come to pass because of what I know now. I am a spiritual being, who has always known from whom my power and blessings have come. I embrace the Universal Consciousness that is God, our ultimate Creator. In fact, of all who inspire me, God tops the list!

As stated in the Bible, *Matthew 7:7-12* *"Ask and it shall be given to you; seek and you will find; knock and the door will be opened to you. For everyone who asks receives; the one who seeks finds; and to the one who knocks, the door will be opened"*

I hope that you enjoy the book for what it offers. I also hope that you can glean something that inspires you to continue this journey of practicing and utilizing the steps, and become successful with the great and magical thing that is, The Law of Attraction.

Many blessings to you on your journey, and happy manifesting!

Annetta L. Hunter

Chapter 1

My Secret Revealed

One of the greatest stories ever told, was no story at all, but reality shared with only the fortunate few who had been exposed to how to believe and achieve their dreams and goals. Throughout history, the secret of living your best life was revealed and practiced by scientists, philosophers, artists, and great thinkers of their day. Call it belief, call it magic, call it faith. Whatever you do call it, it is miraculous!

In 2004, Rhonda Byrne stumbled upon the secret during a very low period in her life. After researching the secret, her life changed! What she learned, she began to practice, and through her belief, and the magic of the law of attraction, her dreams became reality!

I heard of, The Secret movie, in 2006, and was very excited to see what this "Secret" was all about. After watching the movie, I was enthralled with the idea that I could change my life by just thinking and believing in what I wanted my life to be like, then create what they call, a "Vision Board" to help me remember those things. I had practiced Visualization techniques, read books on that subject, and was sure that anything that I had wanted in my life, was mine. For the most part...but after putting into practice some of the steps they said to do, nothing much happened!

I was a little frustrated at that time. I was a new single mother of newborn twins, living with my mother in a cramped little house; in a tiny little town that had nothing to offer me but boredom, I was looking for something to peak my interest and spur on my natural creativity, and to become inspired. After living in Boston, Massachusetts for eight years, living a great and exciting life going to school to obtain my degree in Architecture, enjoying close and wonderful friendships with my peers, a boyfriend who I loved, a dream job in an architectural firm, and traveled whenever I wanted or could afford to do so! One would think that you would not give all that up for the life that I have now, but...I had another dream.

To be a mother; a dream I had always kept in the back of my mind. Finally, at 39, I crashed into my reality, that I was single, in a non-committed relationship, and had become bored with the single life. It became unfulfilling to go out with friends, go to parties, live with other roommates, etc. So, I decided, I wanted to have a baby. If that meant that I would do it on my own with a donor, that's what I would do. But, thoughts of the unknown unsettled me too much to go through with that, so I decided to try to make things work with the present non-committing boyfriend. He had all of the right physical characteristics that told me we would make beautiful and sweet natured babies…but whether or not he would commit finally to me, was not as big an issue as my need to fill the void of motherhood.

When you put the Law of Attraction into play in your life, if you believe with every fiber of your being that that thing you hold most dear will come to pass, and you want it so earnestly, that you make it your daily focus, then miraculously, if it is meant for your good, then that thing should appear.

I began to do just that, and with the help of a good friend, we discussed it all the time and it came to be known as, "The Project". I had such excitement for this project, and nothing was going to stop me from making it a reality! I went to church every Sunday, prayed to God, that he knew my heart and I wanted to give my love so much to a child of my own, I just knew He would not let me down.

As I worked on the project, I knew I could get pregnant, but found that I was unable to carry past 12 weeks. I ended up having 3 miscarriages over two years, until my friend referred me to a female fertility specialist. In my mind, I made the deal with myself, that if I had to have expensive fertility treatments, which were way beyond my budget, that it was just not meant to be, and if whatever she prescribed did not work, then I would accept it and move on. So, I relaxed about the whole thing; which I found is always key! RELAX!

My intention was getting stronger, and little did I know, that timing is everything and a little tweak in my hormonal balance would do the trick! Just a baby aspirin and hormone suppository daily, plus perfect timing was all that it took. And, once again, I became pregnant. But this time, I changed my environment by keeping negativity out of my life. I stayed calm and happy, and became very protective of this pregnancy. I took one day at a time. I worked every day until the day water began leaking. I was petrified. I knew that that could not be good. I went to the emergency room to be checked out. My doctor put me on bed rest for two weeks. During that time, I read the book, "The Power of Positive Thinking". I envisioned the amniotic fluid sac sealing and healing itself, and allowed positive affirmations to fill my mind daily. I kept my activity to the very minimum and checked every day for any trace of the clear leaking fluid. Finally, the leaking subsided and I was I was cleared to return to work. I restricted all activity that would aggravate the situation. I drove to work instead of walking to the bus and taking the train, where I would have to walk a half mile to my office from the train station. I took taxis to meetings in town, where normally I would walk into downtown from my office.

The company was kind enough to pay for the trips, which was a blessing in itself.

I began to get bigger, and the fluid had returned to its normal level in the affected sac. Thank God! I stayed positive, and got to the end of my pregnancy at 32 weeks and delivered my twins! I became the mother of two of the most beautiful little boys that I had ever seen.

And, well, that brings me to where I am today, in this little town of what I called nothingness compared to where I had been, or so I thought. I moved to my hometown, which was supposed to be a temporary situation, and then return to the twin's father to get married, but I needed help from my mother with the babies, because she was such a wonderful mother to me and my sister. I had little experience personally with newborns, or children for that matter, so I needed her guidance and experience! Another reason I moved where I could get help was, their dad worked in Boston, but his home was on the Cape, an hour or so away, so I would be alone with no family near me, no friends down there, so I opted to go back to my home town for a while.

My mother was able to find us a three bedroom home, because her apartment was too tiny and the stairs would not be good for babies or me, seeing as how I had already slipped on them and fell down the stairs a bit while I was in the 4th month of my pregnancy. So, for safety's sake, a one level home was best for her and me.

I had intended to stay for a while, then marry my boyfriend and go back after the babies were a little older and stronger. They were preemies, and one of them had a congenital heart defect and under the care of a Pediatric Cardiologist monthly nearly. Meanwhile, I realized that my relationship with their dad had begun to deteriorate, and after he flew me back East to attend a wedding with him, I found that I did not love him the way that I should if we were to be together forever and raise a happy family. I felt as if something was very off, and I knew divorce would be in my future with him, so, I opted not to go that route in my life, and stay where I was.

So, back to now, the Secret movie prompted me to think about what I wanted going forward, but I was missing something…nothing happened, I did not know there were steps to this whole thing that I had to put into practice, and that is one reason that I am writing this book. I want others to know how to carry out this amazing life building aspect. Not to waste years like I did. Watching movies like, "The Secret", or going to motivating conferences, and reading books, etc. are great! But you must have the steps broken down so that you can achieve what they are talking about, that will make sense to you; is easy to understand, simple to carry out, and you make it a priority in life to change the old way of doing things so that you can create new and exciting scenario's in your life! After nothing much happened for me, I carried on, and I forgot all about it. However, knowing how my "Project" had come to fruition, I knew there was something to it…

Chapter 2

How to Decipher the Secret

Knowing that there is something to all of this Law of Attraction stuff is one thing. But knowing why it really works is another. Well, some of the aspects of it involve quantum physics; it involves metaphysics, nature, faith, positive thinking and believing without failing in your belief. There is actually something even bigger and more basic, yet not fully revealed in the movie, "The Secret" that I will reveal to you in this book.

The definition of The Law of Attraction is that like attracts like. Like-minded people tend to gravitate to one another, but to go a little deeper into this, the like attracts like phenomena lies deep in our sub-conscious minds. For example, what we think, we attract on a sub-conscious level. Or, what we think we are; we are. Whether or not it is a true picture, or not, your mind believes what it is told by your thoughts and it does not know whether or not it is real or not. It perceives and believes the information given to it. Therefore, we must be very, very careful what information we feed our minds. Just like feeding our physical bodies healthy foods to thrive, so should we feed our minds healthy thoughts!

Deciphering the Secret of the Law of Attraction is one of the most fascinating pursuits that I have taken to date! I have immersed myself in it this time...which I will detail in another chapter. Not focusing attention on the negative aspects of what we don't want is key. If we are to be successful with the Law of Attraction, then we would focus on what we want versus what we don't want. As I said before, the Law of Attraction involves very heavy subjects of quantum physics which pulls in scientific proof of like attracting like. Energy: Our bodies are energy, our thoughts are energy, and everything we see in our lives is vibrating energy. The whole universe is energy as well, and this energy works together; works as a whole vibrating pattern of life across all facets of space and time.

Going a little deeper into The Law of Attraction, I have found out that the law is always working. It never ceases. Whatever we think, so shall it be. In fact, I once put so much focus on someone hitting my car; I made it happen without actually meaning to! When I realized what I had done, I was very upset with myself. Luckily, I was not hurt very bad, nor was my car totaled, but it was just as I envisioned in my mind so many times, someone hitting me from behind just as someone had hit my mother a year before, and that is just what happened. Needless to say, I am not envisioning someone hitting my car anymore!

My mother was in a similar situation a year prior to my accident, and she kept saying the whole year before, "I really like the Chrysler 300, I want that car, but I don't want to get it because someone hit my car!" Well, guess what? The Universe was listening, and was playing right into her hands. It was going to give her what she wanted. She did get the car of her dreams, but because someone hit and totaled her car! Again, like me, she is not saying or thinking those negative words anymore…!

So, my question is, why is this not taught to us in school? We learn very little that helps us be successful in living the rest of our lives after we graduate! Why is it, that at 48 years old, nearly more than half of my life is over, that is, if I am blessed to live into my 80's or beyond, am I just now really grasping how to live with intention! Deciphering the Secret to life should be taught from day one! I have 7 year old twin boys now and you better believe I am telling them (when they will listen...!) how to be positive, how to believe that they are worthy and important, and that they are here for a reason; and, to visualize positive situations. My sons are very tender hearted, and get so hurt by anyone who would be mean enough to tease or bully them. I have coached them on how to visualize that person treating them nice, that this person does not bother them any longer and that their days at school are fun and carefree. Often in the mornings before school, we pray to God for them to have a good day, especially if they are feeling anxiety about something that particular day. Invariably, they come home that afternoon and report that they had a good day! We set the tone for the day by envisioning a good protected day!

I will coach them throughout their lives so that this information will become innate and in their younger years they can begin earlier to manifest and enjoy the fruits of knowing the Secret of living a happy, fulfilled life.

That brings me to another wish of how I would like to see the revelation of The Secret fulfilled. I would like school curriculums to be revamped to include courses on living your best life. These courses would include how to truly manage money in the real world, how to save for college, how to save for the future, how to budget not only your money, but your time wisely. These courses would also include Visualization and philosophies of living which include The Law of Attraction. They should teach children from a young age not only the laws of the land, but the laws of the universe. Both are very necessary for living the best life possible in the future. And ultimately, the knowledge that they can create the lives they wish to live!

Chapter 3

Unraveling and Erasing the Negative Thoughts and Behaviors that Hold You Back!

What I have discovered this time around about "The Secret", is what did not work the last time I tried using The Law of Attraction. One of the secrets to "The Secret" I have found is to eradicate negative thought patterns. There is a whole host of negative self-talk that we have lived with our whole lives! As a child, we are told, "No", "Stop Daydreaming", "You Can't", "You are not good enough", "You are not smart enough", and a ton of other trash we tell ourselves, or others tell us into our adulthood. Well, when we start to use the Law of Attraction, there is no room for these words and phrases in our minds! We have to learn how to think positive thoughts, and block or better yet, eradicate the negative thoughts that block you! Say positive affirmations to ourselves that only encourage us to keep the faith and never let up on that faith to believe that what we want, will happen!

Once we begin to practice The Law of Attraction, our negative behaviors also have to be stopped. When we think Big, we cannot act small! Act as if you are, or have that thing you long for; act as if you have the home of your dreams. Start furnishing it in your mind, or when out shopping, look at pieces that would go nicely in your new home. I know it is outlandish, but you are creating your world yourself. Do not limit the process, and inhibit the dream! Step out on faith that it will happen.

Another nugget of truth that I have found to be at play is what I call; and I will interject that this term is my own. "The Law of Your Highest Good". This law has to do with what the God/Universe has in mind for Your Greatest Good. What lesson you may have to learn about a certain dream, wish or goal. And, I have learned that the more you understand the laws and how they work for your greater good; the more relaxed you will be when something does not come to fruition for you. You must accept that it worked out that way because it was in your best interest. Do not go against this law and push something to work your way because you will not benefit from the situation. It may give you satisfaction that you "Made" it work out your way, but in the end, you will find that you should have left well enough alone. The God/Universe still has a plan in place for you to learn all that you can in this life to move on to a higher spiritual plane.

For instance, someone may need a certain amount of money for something. But, things are just not working out to make it happen. That person may push and do something illegal in order to get what they want. That only creates a Karmic debt not only to society, but to your soul! Why create more trouble and lessons for yourself than you already have?!

So, again, as we go through this life of learning, and creating, trust the process and believe that all will work out for your greatest good. We already try to teach our children this lesson; which we try to do when we tell them no, for something we believe is not good for them at that time, or ever, we are already putting this into practice! We just have to remember as adults, God/Universe is also telling us, "No" or "Not Yet" or "Not Now", and we must accept and realize that maybe this was not our experience to have. It is truly freeing when we have attained an understanding of life, and see with new eyes all that we are meant to be!

To reprogram your mind, you have to erase the negative thoughts and phrases that run through our minds all the time. We basically have to re-write the script by replacing words or phrases such as, "Can't", "I'm not good enough", "I'm not smart enough", "Not rich enough".

Replace those words and phrases with, "I Can", "I will learn how", "I'll take classes on or will get a mentor to help me learn", "I have more than enough", "I live in abundance", "I am a money magnet and money comes to me easily", "I am good enough to do whatever I want…" Replacing those negative thoughts with positive thoughts puts a total spin on whatever situation you are talking about, then, the mind accepts that as it hears it over and over.

The mind accepts whatever you tell it. This is the fascinating thing that I am realizing more and more as I study The Law of Attraction. The mind is accepting of whatever you tell it. If you tell it you are broke or that you are sick, that's what it accepts, and the Law of Attraction makes it so. Why would anyone want to attract being broke or sick? But, we do every day! Lacking thoughts keep us in the situation we are in, so stop it! Stop saying things that you do not really want to live! You want to live a life of abundance and good health, trusting that all of your needs will be met.

We also limit our abilities by saying we are not good enough. By believing that we are good enough and taking action to learn a certain skill, practice, or whatever it is you want to be better at, then you become what you think you are. Wouldn't it be better if we believe that we are wonderful? Without being cocky about it, but just genuinely believe you are a good person. You have all that you need to accomplish everything that you wish to do in your life. The entire Universe is working in your favor, and situations work out for your ultimate good. It takes practice to do this, and that is where we learn to immerse ourselves in positivity!

Chapter 4

The Immersion Technique is Key!

As I stated before, I was doing The Law of Attraction the wrong way for years before I learned what it was truly all about. It was very frustrating to me that it did not work when I first saw the movie, "The Secret", but I am glad that I am learning to live by it correctly this time!

What I did not learn before was to immerse myself in learning, listening to practitioners and teachers of The Laws of Attraction, and all the other laws of the universe that there are to learn about on "YouTube" videos. Reading books on the subject, listening to hypnotic messages of positive and success affirmations nightly as I went to sleep, and ultimately, writing this book! I am immersing myself in the subject and I am finding lightness, ease with every situation, love, peace, dreams coming true, and goals met. It is exciting to see this new realization unfolding before my eyes!

Lately, I see butterflies everywhere I go! I think the universe is trying to tell me that I am on the right track. I have been in the cocoon for too long, and my beautiful butterfly wings of many colors are beginning to spread and dry from the wet chrysalis that contained them. It is exciting!

Now, it is very easy to do one thing every day once you begin to live by the rules of The Law of Attraction. Do one little thing daily to remind you of it. Read an affirmation that you create that speaks volumes to your soul! Create a Vision Board with all the dreams you hope to acquire in this lifetime. They do not have to be material things; they can be to increase your spirituality, to stay at peace, to be more giving to those in need, etc. You make it what you want your life to be, but it must have strong emotion attached to it for it to take wings and fly!. Make sure that it feels good to you and brings you excitement or peace. There should be nothing that limits you and your dreams. Remember, you do not have to figure out exactly "How" you will attain, or attract those things; you just have to believe the end result has been satisfied and you are happy with the outcome.

Another golden nugget on the things we wish for are: Whenever you dream or wish to attain something, be sure that it is for the right reasons; for your highest good. If you wish for something that will harm another, that thing may come to pass, but wreaks havoc with our karmic life. If what you wish to attain is held by another, be happy for that person and that they have that wonderful thing; for it was meant for them. But, if you say that you are happy for them having it, the universe boomerangs it back to you, and you say, that you would like something like that or better. In that way, you are not trying to harm another to get what they have!

We should live our best lives, dream big, and be grateful for everything, then; you will find things that you want come easier. You begin to notice that what you hold dear and precious will be enjoyed more fully. Remember also to live in the moment you are in and be happy right where you are! We all like to daydream, think and dream about our futures, but remember to relish the moment you are in. In other words, regard your "Now" as well as future events you wish to live. Because at some point in the past, you were hoping for the now you are living presently, so don't miss it!

Also, as you are on this process of immersion, make it a challenge to yourself to let it become a habit, and that you do something, read something; listen to something that keeps you on this good vibrational pattern daily! You actually want this to be second nature after a while, so that you never forget your goals, what you are accomplishing with your mind. And ultimately, have fun with it, do not stress over it. Stressing creates a regression in your momentum and we need to only focus on what pushes us forward in this quest. As I mentioned previously, I would reveal something that was not fully explained in "The Secret" movie, and that was it!

Chapter 5

It's A Mindset...
Get your mind set to take Action!

When I say that it is a mindset...get your mind set to take action! I mean, you really do have to clear your mind of all negative thoughts. You have to prepare yourself for what I call a "self-study" of yourself. Your purpose in this life is important for you to tap into; if it is nothing more than doing what makes you happiest, and filling your life with that. As long as it does not hurt anyone, you are ok! But, truly doing the things that bring you joy are what create the optimum vibration for your spirit. We are all part of a whole continuum of consciousness that never stops working, moving, developing. We need to get a better understanding of what part we are playing in that, and when you have discovered those things that make you happy, keep moving and creating your life to suit that.

For instance, someone who is working at a job that they hate; they may have to stay inside for 8 hours a day, but they love nature and yearn to be involved with nature more, so what they need to do is find what will fulfill that yearning, and that provides a living as well! We do not have to stay stuck in the usual 9 to 5 grind. We have to be willing to step out on faith, visualize your perfect job, career, business, or mode of study; research it, and visualize some more. With some intentional action, doors will open, key people will be introduced to you that get you one step closer to your dream, or at the very least, try that thing out for a while to see if that will be a good fit, and feels right inside. We cannot rely on the status quo, the drudgery of "Must-do's" that our parents and their parents have passed down to us. I remember growing up in the 70's during the free love, and freedom of living movement. People were happy; they felt more in tune with who they really were; at least it seemed that that was true. Maybe it was partly due to the free flowing herbs that helped them along as well! But, I tell you, you can get to that nirvana without using illegal drugs or other paraphernalia. We have to go within more than we ever did before, love ourselves and tune into your higher power. Have moments of peace and quiet to reflect. If you are good at meditation, you can get there a lot quicker. If you need help, YouTube has a lot of guided short or long meditations with beautiful music and visuals to help you on your way. So, go there, make a daily habit of finding that inner peace to find out who you are, what you want and live the greatest life you can!

Take one step every day; put your goals into bite sized pieces so that you can feel assured that that thing is attainable, because the steps are easy. Then, by time you have accomplished the goal, put into place a larger goal and go about it the same way! I learned a fantastic lesson once during my high school years in drafting class. Our teacher told us to draw an oil well pump. I looked at the picture and all of the intricate parts and pieces that had to be drawn, and how big the pump was. Immediately, I thought, I can never draw that! It's too much! Then, a little voice in my head said, "It's not too big, you only perceive it that way. If you take one small part and draw that, then, draw the next small part attached to that, and so on, and so on, then you will have drawn the whole picture!" Now, the words I heard in my mind were simple, and the message I remembered always and applied to every similar situation I encountered in my life. When you take anything in small pieces, the big problems of life, the goals we set out to achieve, the college degree we want, or the business we want to start is possible!

Now, remember, that these words are nice, but you have to do something with them! You must take ACTION! Let's pull apart the word, ACT – I—ON and rearrange it:

ACT: To Do Something

I: Me, I must do that something!

ON: Whatever it is you want, act on it!

Furthermore, you can mix up the word we pulled apart to say, "I Act On" So, let's go do it, act on that thing you want daily. Writing a book; just like the one I am writing now. I've never completed a book, a short story that I started, but I am changing that habit of non-completion In my life by writing something nearly every day. I write whenever I get inspired, when I know, the only way that I am going to achieve this goal is to do something on it daily, no matter how small it is, I am practicing what I preach by writing a little at a time. And, I am seeing that it is working! I hope you find my antidote to overcoming not getting started, or not finishing a project helpful! As well as taking on a big task, whatever it is, and attack in in bits and pieces and soon you will have achieved that big task to completion!

Chapter 6

Creating Your World...
Create the Vision First!

What do you want? Simply put; what is it that you want, that is important enough for you to daydream about constantly? Is it a house, that sexy car! Is it having children, or that perfect mate? Whatever it is, it is important to you! We choose the things we want in life to help us grow and learn life lessons, or to have experiences that will expand our knowledge and strengthen us as human beings.

We create our world with our choices. Even the bad things unfortunately; we have chosen them. But, because you now know about The Secret, and The Law of Attraction, you can stop making bad choices and turn around a bad situation before it gets too bad! We must watch the words that come out of our mouths and play like ticker tape in our minds, not only to ourselves, but to others!

The negatives, the doomed scenarios we talk about or predict, all create the lives we are living, so instead, create positive visions and speak positive phrases on everything! If you think a negative word or phrase about something, before you let it out of your mouth, turn it around and say it to reflect a positive outcome!

When I decided that I wanted the experience of becoming a mother, wanting a child, I set out with intention! I had three miscarriages, but I did not let them ruin me, or my dream. I knew or eventually found out that even though I could get pregnant, there was something that needed to be fixed in order to hold the pregnancy! One thing that I believe whole-heartedly is that people are in your life for a reason. My friend who I confided in about my wanting to be a mother was integral in helping me achieve my goal because she knew of a female fertility specialist who she suggested I go see. Well, what she tried with me was a very simple thing, and it worked! I also stopped being or feeling desperate about it. That is also very key to making The Law of Attraction work for you! Stop acting and being desperate. After you have tried everything and you still have not succeeded, apparently there is some tweaking that needs to be done. Look at what you have done in the past. Decipher what seemed to work and what did not quite get you the outcome you were looking for. Test out another approach and decide to be very relaxed and at peace about it, step away from it for a while, and you may just find, that that's when it comes to fruition!

If you want to be rich, do not lament about being poor! All you will get is more of being poor versus becoming rich. Remember, that The Law of Attraction is: What you focus on, you attract. So, why would anyone focus on being poor? Especially, when what you really want is the exact opposite!

Now, when you create your vision, be specific. Intricate in fact, so that when you picture it in your mind, you have all of the details filled in. Being general will get you general results. It may be close to it, but not exactly it! So, focus on the details, make it so real in your mind that you could feel it, touch it and act as if it is.

In fact, "Acting as if" is also a key element to success in your quest to realizing your dreams. I take showers in my beautiful home all the time, in my mind, I picture the marble bathroom, the Romanesque tiles in the shower stall, the glass wall and door of the shower, the shiny silver faucets and handles put me into a zone of belief that that house is out there waiting on me, and my bathroom is exactly as I have envisioned it. I feel it, I see the light coming from the window, and I see the light fixtures illuminating the bathroom, and I feel relaxed and happily living in luxury. It's amazing! The mind will send you on momentary trips of bliss when you are creative and play with this visioning. Make it fun, make it real to you and it will be!

Another way to create your vision is to cut out pictures of the things you want, and post them in places that you will see it daily. Like the bathroom mirror. Every morning you wake up and see that picture, and pretty soon, it's second nature for the mind to expect it, it sees it in your mind, and your eyes see it daily to remind you of what you want, especially helpful when you may have other distracting thoughts on your mind that have pushed down the positive things.

There is a woman who strongly believed that she was going to win the lottery. She even said how much she was going to win, and talked about it with enthusiasm to her close family members. She believed it with feeling, and wrote the figure on a piece of paper, folded it and stuck it under her pillow.

What she was doing was a five step process:

1. She had the Vision
2. She gave it strong emotion
3. Acted as if
4. She wrote it down
5. She gave it to the Universe

A lot of people miss the boat when they do not practice each step in concert. You can have the vision, but may not give it the right amount of emotion, you may act as if, but neglect to write it down and keep a visual of it, then some may not let it go. Believing on the thing you want, then letting it out into the Universe and allowing it to sink into your unconscious mind, for it to work on it for you, is a key element as well!

Now, the only thing that is missing in the five steps is "Action". Most everything that you want requires action. What if she did all those steps but neglected buying a lottery ticket?! How ridiculous would that be? So, do not forget to take the action that whatever you want requires!

Chapter 7

Vision Boards and Goals Oh My!

What is a Vision Board? Well, if you have looked at the movie," The Secret", then you already know and was impressed with John Assaraf's story of a vision board he had created years before he realized that the vision had become his reality. He had pinned a house that he loved onto his vision board. About 5 years later, he had moved into a house he had bought and renovated, and his son happened by in his office and sat on a box of his vision boards. After his son asked what was in the box, he began to explain, but because his son was very young, decided that showing his son was better, so he pulled out one of the boards, and immediately his eye caught the picture of his dream home, and he began to cry, because he realized that he was in the dream home on the board! His dream of owning the home on the board had come true; however, he did not even realize it until then; I believe because it had sunk so deep into his unconscious mind, it was no longer at the forefront in his conscious mind, except taking the necessary actions to making it his reality years later!

It was an amazing story, and I really love to hear stories like that because it inspires me to keep pushing forward, or to "allow" my dreams to become my reality! And, I want to encourage you as well! I will give you the best information on how to create a Vision Board that will really work, and know that if you follow these steps, they will happen!

1. First, get a board. The board can be cork, foam core board, poster board, or whatever background medium you like, even a computer screen! Today, they have electronic vision boards, called mind movies, and so forth that can go with you wherever you go! I created one of those, and then I printed it off so that I could post a copy in my bathroom, and in my bedroom and in my office. All the places that I spend a lot of time at one point or so in my day.

2. Next, gather images of inspirational emotion filled words, images, and phrases to post on your board. A very important point to make is you must have an emotional connection or resonance with the images and words for this to work. So, do not waste your time putting this board together and put it in a closet or under the bed and forget it. You must "Feel" something strong for all elements of your board so that when you look at it, it will remind you on a deeper level of what you want.

3. After putting the images on the board, post the board where you will see it daily. You might place it where you work on a wall where you see it for 8 hours a day. Post it on a wall in your bedroom where when you wake up, that is the first thing you see and at night, the last thing you see, so that you go to sleep with those visions in your mind.

4. Commit it to the Universe or God to deliver to you, but also, take some action on those things. If you want to be an award winning Author, but never write a book, that is

probably not going to come true because you are not taking action by writing a book of some kind. Then, get it published! No one will buy a book that you don't allow them to see, so follow through on the action and keep pushing it!

5. Believe. Trust and believe that your dreams will come to pass. Have gratitude in your heart for all that you have presently, and all that you "believe" you have presently.

6. You might also want to make sure that you are in good physical and mental health. Eat healthy foods, exercise, meditate, and drink lots of water. You have to be ready for these good things to come to you, and healthy enough to enjoy them!

7. Mentally, and spiritually, you need to be in a good vibrational place to manifest your dreams without having blockages such as resentments, hatreds, jealousy, anger and negative feelings about anything, because all of those feelings and emotions put you out of alignment with the

goodness of the universe. You must let go of those bitter feelings and concentrate on wishing others well, encouraging others who you might not have gotten along with or have done you wrong in the past. Be happy for someone who has something that you want instead of being jealous, because the emotions of happiness you have for someone else come back to you and bring you those things in which you were jealous of! These negative emotions also make you sick, which negates number 6!

If you truly believe in those things, and give them to God / Universe to bring them to you in concert with your actions, vibration, and positivity in every area of your life and with every person in your life, you will be amazed at what transpires!

Chapter 8

Breaking Free to Finally Achieve your Dreams!

I mentioned "Vibration" at the end of the last chapter. I would like to expand on what I mean by that term. It is difficult for a lot of us to believe that we are more than our physical bodies, but we are. Our bodies are merely containers of our soul / spirit. When we leave this world, our spirit joins the collective consciousness / God, and we become our "whole" spirit being once again. We vibrate at a much greater level as our "whole spirit being" because we are all knowing, and complete, exuding love and happiness. I would like to operate at that level the majority of my life if I could while still living! It takes practice to get on that higher vibration level, but we can do it! How will you know when you have gotten there? Well, our dreams of what we want resonate on a certain vibration, so that when we get to the place where we match that vibration, those things come to us in our reality! Then you will know that you have achieved that certain vibration you seek.

In other words, our emotions are the driving force of our spirit, or what I will call here, your vibrational being. To be able to achieve the dreams, goals or whatever you desire, your vibrational being must be in alignment with that desire. We can achieve better results of The Law Attraction by being at one with the vibrational being within us. Again, we are two beings; our physical body beings; and our vibrational beings. The more we are at one with that inner being, the more successful we will be in our lives, because we know what makes us happy, we know what brings us inner peace. We know what will send us into the stratosphere of bliss!

How can we sense the vibrational being that we are? How do you feel when you are in love? We feel free, we are flying! Everything you see is beautiful, and you are happy beyond words! We are overjoyed inside, and when we are, we are also feeling at one with our vibrational being. That vibrational being wants only joy, happiness and peace for you, but as physical beings, we lower that vibration with ego, greed, negative thought limitations, worry, and stress.

Stepping out on faith is sometimes hard for us. We are impatient, wanting to see in the physical now, what you want; so that you can believe you have it! Not believing you have already what you want, is a challenge we must overcome if we are to obtain those special things. It will take some practice to stay mindful that what you ask for, you already have, even though it has not physically materialized. If we can get to that place, you are there in your oneness with your vibrational being. Break free from the wants of the physical body and get ready to achieve your dreams by aligning with the universe and believing you already have what you seek. Feel it physically, see it visually, smell it, taste it, experience the feeling of having it, and you will!

Chapter 9

Measure Your Success...
Be Grateful for Everything

Do you ever think about things that you have wanted in your life, and realize as you take stock in them, that you have manifested quite a lot of what you have wanted in your life? If that is so, then it might be a helpful practice to keep a "Gratitude Journal". This journal chronicles each item you desire in life. It keeps you mindful that God hears your prayers, or that the Universe is giving you your hearts' desire! The way that I have kept my Gratitude Journal is to write down the date; and the thing that I would like to have manifested in my life. I leave space on the other side by dividing the sheet in half with a line, then after attaining it, write down the date it manifested and thank God / Universe for bringing it to me. This journal can also help you realize and measure your success at practicing the Law of Attraction!

If by chance, you have not gotten a lot of the things you want, this practice is also beneficial; because it helps you practice gratitude for the little, as well as practice gratitude for the multitude. We should always be thankful for everything in our lives. Our health, our families, our homes, and even the rickety old car you drive, and many of the other things we seemingly take for granted.

Sincerity is also very important. We have to practice gratitude with a sincere heart and mind. Playing at it is no good. God knows, and "He don't like ugly!" As they say. So, be sincere in your thanking him for every little thing, and treat it well. Act like you are grateful for it. I tell my sons all the time, to treat their things with care, and those things will last, and maybe you will get more because you have taken care of those things. Do they listen? Sometimes; or most times; they are only 7, so in time...!

Now, let's look at your attitude about gratitude! We need to have a good attitude period, but even when we do not get the things we are seeking right away, we must keep an attitude of gratitude, because it does not mean you will not get that thing you seek, it's just not time for it to manifest just yet, and or you are not a vibrational match yet. And, if you are truly practicing The Law of Attraction, in your mind, you already have that thing; it just has not materialized! But, it's on its way, so stay grateful in its absence and always believe that it is coming.

Chapter 10

Pass it On!
Share the Secret with Others

Passing it on, and sharing The Secret with others about The Law of Attraction, is so very important. I say, it especially for our children. I have encountered children who somehow naturally believe that things will not work out for them. They had a bad attitude about positive thinking! And, I also discovered that their father had the same attitude! Even when a child does not have daily contact or regular contact with that person, they can exhibit the same attitude. I was shocked when I discovered this within my child! I am about the most positive person you will meet! And, shocked that my son who is only around his father once a year for a visit back East, exhibits the same negative attitudes that he and his other child, who I also interacted with in her formative years, actually had the same attitude! Then my child, almost verbatim said the same things that she did about their ability to do something, or believe something good about themselves!

So, I have some work to do with him! As I said, he is 7, and every opportunity I have to reinforce positive thinking, I do it, and so should all parents of children who are more down on themselves than they need to be. The key too, is that parents / guardians of children need to have a positive believing attitude in themselves, and exhibit those attitudes in the way that they live their lives! Ultimately, passing on the attitude of belief in your dreams, gratitude attitudes, and believing that you create your realities to your children, will not only affect them, but it affects the people around them as they grow up, their children, and then the community they live in, and so on, and so on!

I am passing on the information that I have learned all my life from my mother. She has always been able to manifest anything that she wanted. If there was a car she wanted, if there was a house she wanted, she got it. What she did was put the intention out there, saw the object of her affection, and we drove by it all the time, dreaming that we lived in that particular house, or we owned a particular car and totally bought into the idea that it was ours! Then, miraculously it was! Now, there was action behind the belief, and I will put the whole Law of Attraction recipe together at the end of this book, but as I have said, action is a key component to some things that you want to manifest! You cannot sit back and wait for it to appear in front of you, you have to do some work!

One of my dreams was to write a book to help those who have never received information like this in their lives, so that they can use it to make their lives better, and to believe that it is possible to actually have a big dream and realize it! I dreamed of going around to locations where I met people in the public who were down trodden, or unfulfilled in their lives, and share this information with them, by handing them this book. I want to share this knowledge with everyone! Then also, I want to befriend others who believe in the principles of The Law of

Attraction, creating a network of support and exchange of creative ideas with one another! I am going to do these things, because now, I have the book! I want to take my show on the road so to speak as well, and give talks to people who really need it so that they can get this information for themselves and use it! Especially to schools where our future generations can start thinking good thoughts about themselves, staying on a high vibrational level, and make their realities everything they want to make it from the start, and not waste time trying to figure it out! I kind of knew about these things when I was younger, but I did not have a process and something to call it really. I knew that we could see something, like a house we wanted to move to, and think about it being ours all the time, and believe it, and somehow, it came about. But, think about how powerful you could be in creating your great life, by actually using this with intention. Knowing the keys to making your reality wonderful! Knowing the keys of how emotion plays such a vital part in creating good and bad scenarios in your life.

Also, how your actions create karmic reactions that you want to be sure are positive and not negative!

Interestingly, I have discovered when I do use The Law of Attraction for little things, they can manifest quite quickly, but the process seems to be very subtle, and it just works! There is not a lot of energy put into allowing the thing I want to manifest, but what process I have used, is almost imperceptible, that I am almost surprised at how easy it was! I feel a bit detached from it, and then it appears.

Detachment is another key element in practicing The Law of Attraction. Once you have visualized what you want, detach from it. Let it sink into the unconscious mind where the work begins. Meanwhile you take the steps, by taking action, and oftentimes without the realization that that is what you are doing, to help a manifestation along. In other words, you have to stop dwelling on the thing and allow the process to work!

Bonus Chapter

The Law of Attraction Recipe

After a lot of research on this subject, I have come to find out that practicing The Law of Attraction is a host of steps, methods, training of your thoughts and preparation to believe. There is a process that you go through, that after lots of practice, it just becomes second nature! That's the best part, because then, you find yourself thinking that you want this certain something, and all of a sudden or in time, there it is! I have had this happen repeatedly. And, if you become very aware of what you are doing in the beginning, it is fun to see your intentions come to you in the physical form as you allow them through knowing the keys to this incredible power.

In my research on the subject of The Law of Attraction, I have studied and researched many authorities on the subject of manifestation, this is a small list of the following teachers today who are well known in the Law of Attraction circles; they are:

~ Brian Tracy
~ John Assaraf
~ Wayne Dyer
~ Bob Proctor
~ Ester and Jerry Hicks aka: "Abraham"

The Law of Attraction recipe is made up of specific ingredients. However, as you learn more and more, varying items can be added or subtracted to make it work for you!

1. 1 cups Visualization
2. 3/4 cups of action
3. 1/2 cup of Clearing the blocks
4. 1 ½ cups of Blind faith
5. 1 cup of Acting as if
6. ½ cup of Release

Mix all ingredients together with love, emotion and positive thinking until completely incorporated into your mind. Pour into your gratitude pan, detach from it and give it time to bake until the timer says it is ready! Share with as many as you can find.

Enjoy!

I hope that my words bring you encouragement, inspiration, a reason to take action and belief that your actions will bring you all that you desire. Remember to share this universal life creating power with the ones you love!

The End

www.ingramcontent.com/pod-product-compliance
Lightning Source LLC
Chambersburg PA
CBHW061252040426
42444CB00010B/2362